Take Ten Years

1960s

KEN HILLS

Evans

EVANS BROTHERS LIMITED

Contents

The pictures on page 4 show
John F. Kennedy
Yuri Gagarin
The shooting of Kennedy
US troops in South Vietnam
Ian Smith at Victoria Falls

The pictures on page 5 show
Mao Tse-tung
Francis Chichester's *Gipsy Moth IV*
Troops training in Biafra
Demonstration in Prague 1968
The footprint of Neil Armstrong's first step on the moon
A paper mini dress

Introduction

World affairs in the sixties were dominated by the enmity between the two superpowers, Soviet Russia and the United States of America. Between them, they held stocks of nuclear weapons capable of destroying the entire earth 20 times over. For a few terrifying days in October 1962, war between the two superstates over nuclear bases in Cuba seemed almost inevitable. But as the rest of the world looked on helplessly, the two sides paused to consider the fearful consequences of a nuclear conflict. Both agreed to compromise, and a war which might have ended life on earth was averted.

Wars were seldom out of the headlines in the sixties. As the decade wore on, America was sucked deeper and deeper into the Vietnam conflict. The age-old enmity between Israelis and Arabs boiled over into a violent six-day clash which the Israelis won with astonishing ease. Other wars afflicted Nigeria and Cyprus.

The sixties were a decade of protest. In America, opposition to the Vietnam War, and the struggle for civil rights by black people, led to violent clashes. In South Africa, many died as the ruling whites cracked down on attempts by the non-whites to win equality and justice. In the Communist world, Soviet troops ruthlessly suppressed protest in Czechoslovakia. In Germany a wall was built across Berlin to prevent discontented citizens in the Communist East from leaving in search of greater freedom and prosperity in the West.

Numbers of young people in the West dropped out of normal life as a reaction to the violence of the times and turned to a way of life based on peace and love. They became the hippie generation and they influenced millions more with their ideas and fashions. Their feelings were expressed by the words and music of groups like the Beatles and individuals such as Bob Dylan and Joan Baez.

The decade ended with the supreme triumph of science and technology, landing the first human beings on the moon, and returning them safely to earth.

YEARS	WORLD AFFAIRS
1960	USA-USSR summit meeting in Paris Congolese independence Nigerian independence
1961	East Germans flee to the West East Germans close border at Berlin US and USSR test nuclear weapons
1962	USSR ships missiles to Cuba USA blockades Cuba Threat of war averted
1963	Assassination of J. F. Kennedy
1964	Lyndon B. Johnson elected US president Palestine Liberation Organization founded China tests atom bomb
1965	Rhodesia declares independence Sanctions imposed on Rhodesia
1966	Cultural Revolution in China India elects Indira Gandhi
1967	Tension in Middle East Six-Day War gives Israel new territory Colonels' junta seizes Greece
1968	Czechoslovakia's Prague spring crushed Richard Nixon elected US President
1969	

WARS & REVOLTS	PEOPLE	EVENTS
Sharpeville Massacre Revolt in Algeria	Gary Powers admits spying mission J. F. Kennedy elected as US President Verwoerd shot in South Africa	US spyplane shot down over USSR Rome Olympic Games
British troops defend Kuwait Arab League guards Kuwait Bay of Pigs Cuban coup fails	Yuri Gagarin in space Eichmann condemned to death	J. F. Kennedy sworn in as US President
Race riots in Mississippi	John Glenn becomes the first American in space Marilyn Monroe dies Nelson Mandela jailed American painter Andy Warhol exhibits Pop Art	Coventry Cathedral re-dedicated First hovercraft service
	Profumo scandal in London Pope John XXIII dies	Great Train Robbery Beeching Report axes British trains
US send troops to Vietnam	Martin Luther King wins Nobel Peace Prize Mandela jailed for life Nehru dies	Tokyo Olympic Games Cassius Clay wins heavyweight boxing title
Race riots in Alabama, USA Race riots in Watts, USA More US troops sent to Vietnam	Sir Winston Churchill dies Beatles are awarded MBEs	Civil rights demonstration in USA End of death penalty in UK
US offensive in Vietnam Australian troops go to Vietnam	Francis Chichester knighted Verwoerd murdered	Aberfan tragedy in Wales England wins world cup Labour wins UK election
Nigerian civil war Vietnam war continued Six-Day war between Israel and Arab states	Donald Campbell dies in accident Sir Francis Chichester sails home	De Gaulle blocks UK entry to Common Market Concorde unveiled Festival of Love Heart transplant
Riots in US after King's murder Nigerian war continues; Biafrans defeated	Martin Luther King murdered Yuri Gagarin dies Bobby Kennedy murdered	Mexico Olympic Games US astronaut orbits moon
	Neil Armstrong and Edwin Aldrin walk on the moon	*Apollo 11* mission lands men on the moon North Sea oil discovered

1960

SUMMIT RAISES HOPES FOR PEACE

May 2, Moscow In two weeks' time the two superpower leaders, Premier Khrushchev of Soviet Russia and President Eisenhower of the United States, will meet in Paris. Their task is to try to end the distrust and enmity between their countries, called the Cold War. Both countries have nuclear weapons, and conflict between these nations seems to threaten to plunge the world into war.

RUSSIANS SHOOT DOWN US PLANE

May 5, Moscow The Russians claim that the plane they shot down on May 1 was a US spyplane flying over Soviet territory. The American State Department denies that the plane was spying. The US announcement maintains that the plane was engaged in weather research, but was blown off course and accidently strayed across the Soviet border. It carried cameras to photograph the clouds, say the Americans.

PILOT ADMITS HE WAS SPYING

May 10, Moscow The Soviet authorities have released pictures of the wreckage of the US U-2 plane shot down last week. They have also produced the pilot, Gary Powers, who survived the crash unharmed. Powers has admitted that when he was shot down he was on a spying mission between Pakistan and Norway.

The accused spy pilot, Gary Powers, sits in the dock at his trial in Moscow.

PARIS PEACE TALKS COLLAPSE

May 17, Paris The talks here have broken up in angry confusion. The United States refuses to apologize for the spy flight. The Russians have chosen to make the most of America's refusal and are using it as an excuse for wrecking the talks. Mr. Khrushchev showed his contempt for President Eisenhower by stopping in the streets of Paris to hand out ball-point pens to passing children when he should have been attending a meeting. It seems that the Cold War between the Communist East and the Capitalist West is colder than ever.

PROTESTERS DIE IN SOUTH AFRICA

Heavily armed police move among bodies of dead Africans outside the prison at Sharpeville.

March 21, Johannesburg Today 67 people were killed, and nearly 200 injured, at Sharpeville, an African township south of Johannesburg. Thousands of black Africans had gathered to protest against the hated pass laws, which require Africans to carry identity cards at all times. When stones were thrown, the police panicked and opened fire. More Africans have been gunned down at a similar demonstration in Langa township near Cape Town.

STATE OF EMERGENCY DECLARED IN SOUTH AFRICA

March 30, Pretoria Unrest continues in South Africa. Black Africans are demanding the release of their leaders, imprisoned for opposing the apartheid laws which keep black people in subjection to the whites. The police have been given powers to arrest and detain anyone whom they suspect may be a danger to the State.

AMERICA ELECTS YOUNGEST PRESIDENT

Nov 9, Washington Only 120,000 votes separated the Democrat John F. Kennedy from his Republican opponent Richard Nixon in today's presidential election. JFK, as he is known, is 43 and due to become the youngest president ever to lead the United States.

THREAT OF CIVIL WAR IN ALGERIA

Jan 24, Algiers Several thousand European settlers in Algeria have come out in revolt against the French government's plan to grant independence to the colony. The rebels are French, as are the troops stationed in Algeria. So far, the army commanders have refrained from ordering their men into action against their fellow countrymen.

ALGERIAN REVOLT CRUMBLES

Feb 1, Paris The revolt that threatened to tear Algeria apart has collapsed. President de Gaulle appeared on television two days ago. He appealed to the French army in Algeria to remain loyal to him and to France. The de Gaulle magic worked. The troops have forced the rebels to take down their barricades and surrender.

BIRTH CONTROL PILL

Dec 1, London Women in America and Britain will soon be able to buy a pill to prevent unwanted pregnancies. Scientists in America first discovered how to make the pill in 1951. Following trials on thousands of women, doctors are now confident that the contraceptive pill is safe. It will go on sale next month.

NEWS IN BRIEF . . .

RECORD ROME OLYMPICS

Sept 4, Rome A record 5337 competitors took part in the Rome Olympics, making them the biggest ever. The USA and the USSR topped the medal lists, but the star of the games was the Australian middle-distance runner Herb Elliott, who outclassed his rivals. He finished the 1500 metres race three seconds clear of the rest of the field, in world-record time.

US PILOT FOUND GUILTY

Aug 19, Moscow A Soviet court has found Gary Powers guilty and sentenced him to ten years in prison. Powers was the pilot of the camera-carrying US plane shot down over Soviet territory earlier this year. The episode was the cause of the failure of the Paris peace talks.

INDEPENDENCE FOR NIGERIA

Oct 1, Lagos At midnight last night, Nigeria became independent. Nigeria was Britain's largest colony and with nearly 50 million people is Africa's most populous country.

The Australian Herb Elliott wins the men's 1500 m at the Rome Olympics.

BRITAIN ENDS CALL-UP

Dec 31, London The last group of 18-year-old men to serve compulsory National Service receive their call-up notices today. They will serve in the army, navy or air force for 18 months. From now on, Britain's armed forces will have to rely on volunteers to fill their ranks.

SOUTH AFRICAN PREMIER SHOT

April 9, Johannesburg Prime Minister Verwoerd has been shot and wounded. His attacker is a wealthy white farmer named David Pratt. The shooting follows last month's disturbances in which hundreds of black Africans were killed or wounded as they protested against the apartheid laws. Doctors here say that Prime Minister Verwoerd will recover but white South Africans are shocked that this act of violence should have been carried out by a white man.

ARMY ACTS TO END CONGO CHAOS

Sept 15, Leopoldville Army leader Colonel Joseph Mobutu has seized power in Belgium's former colony of the Congo. Parliament has been shut down and its leaders arrested. The Congo became independent on June 30 this year, under the leadership of Patrice Lumumba, and has been in a state of violent disorder ever since. There was an army rebellion, and both Belgian and United Nations forces were mobilized in an attempt to regain stability. Colonel Mobutu blames the politicians for the chaos in which the Congo finds itself. He intends to appoint a new government to restore law and order.

1961

EAST GERMANS FLEE TO WEST

July 31, Berlin East Germans at the rate of 30,000 a month are seeking a new life in the West. They make the crossing in Berlin, which is divided into sectors controlled by the Russians, the Americans, the British and the French. There is a steady drain of skilled workers and professional people leaving the drab conditions in the East to seek a new life in prosperous West Germany. Not only is this a bad advertisement for Communism, it also damages the economy of East Germany.

The East Germans build up the wall between East and West Berlin at a gate where there was only barbed wire. Families are being torn apart as the border is closed.

COMMUNISTS CLOSE BERLIN BORDER

Aug 13, Berlin Early this morning, East German border guards closed the crossing points between East and West Berlin. Troops are laying down rolls of barbed wire along the entire frontier running through the city. All unauthorized travel across the border has been stopped.

A WALL DIVIDES EAST FROM WEST

Aug 23, Berlin A wall has replaced the rolls of barbed wire across Berlin. Snaking from north to south, a concrete barrier 2m (7 ft) high now separates the two parts of the city. The wall is backed by anti-tank ditches in many places.

KENNEDY SWORN IN AS US PRESIDENT

Jan 20, Washington   John F. Kennedy became the 35th President of the United States at an impressive ceremony today, here in the nation's capital. Millions watched on television as he called upon his fellow citizens to work for the good of America. "Ask not what your country can do for you;" he said, "ask what you can do for your country."

The new president makes his inaugural speech.

Yuri Gagarin in *Vostok 1*, in which he made the first manned orbit of the earth.

RUSSIAN LAUNCHED INTO SPACE

April 12, Moscow   The Russians have announced an extraordinary technological triumph. Earlier today, 27-year old Major Yuri Gagarin landed safely after flying round the world in space. His historic flight in the spaceship *Vostok 1* lasted 108 minutes. The USSR has thus beaten the Americans in the race to put a human being into space.

SUPERPOWERS STEP UP NUCLEAR TESTING

Sept 5, Moscow   Over the last five days the Russians have exploded three nuclear bombs at their test range in Siberia. This action has provoked the Americans into resuming their own nuclear test programme. The US bombs will be set off deep down in the Nevada desert to avoid spreading radioactive fall-out.

FIASCO AT BAY OF PIGS

April 20, Havana, Cuba The attempt by anti-Communist Cubans to overthrow the government of Fidel Castro has ended in disaster. The invasion force which landed at the Bay of Pigs three days ago has been destroyed. All 1400 of them have been either killed or captured. The Soviet government has accused the Americans of aiding the invasion.

ARABS TO GUARD KUWAIT

Sept 19, Kuwait City Troops from Saudi Arabia and other Arab states have arrived to take over the defence of Kuwait. They replace the British force which was rushed here last July to head off a threatened invasion by Kuwait's neighbour Iraq.

These British soldiers on guard in Kuwait will soon be replaced by a joint Arab force.

NEWS IN BRIEF . . .

KENNEDY FOUNDS PEACE CORPS

March 1, Washington Young men and women in America can now join an organization called the Peace Corps, which President Kennedy unveiled today. Peace Corps volunteers will work on development projects in Third World countries.

MORE US TROOPS FOR VIETNAM

Nov 14, Washington Over the next two years, the number of US troops serving in South Vietnam will rise from 1000 to 16,000. Communist guerrillas from North Vietnam now control large areas in the South.

Ham and his nurse before the historic flight into space.

CHIMP IN SPACE

Jan 31, Cape Canaveral, USA American scientists have sent a chimpanzee named Ham 240 km (150 miles) into space. Ham was blasted off in a Mercury space capsule on an 18-minute flight as part of America's programme to overtake Russia's lead in the space race.

EICHMANN TO DIE FOR MASS MURDER

Dec 15, Jerusalem Ex-Nazi officer Adolf Eichmann has been condemned to death for his part in the killing of millions of Jews in World War II. Eichmann fled to Argentina at the end of the war and hid there under a false name. Israeli agents found him, arrested him and brought him secretly to Israel.

1962

THE CUBAN MISSILE CRISIS

Oct 16, Washington The Soviet Union has been shipping weapons of war to Cuba ever since the Bay of Pigs invasion. Now the latest spy plane pictures show that the USSR is building rocket launch pads on Cuba. From there, nuclear missiles could be launched to hit the USA. President Kennedy and his advisors are considering most urgently what they should do to put an end to this new and deadly threat.

CUBAN CRISIS DEEPENS

Oct 25, Washington Ships of the US navy have warned off a Russian convoy heading for Cuba. Twelve vessels thought to be carrying nuclear weapons turned round and sailed away before they could be boarded by the Americans. Meanwhile, work on the Cuban missile sites goes on. A nuclear war between the USA and the Soviet Union is now feared to be a very real possibility. Tension is very high as the world watches and waits.

1962 CUBAN MISSILE CRISIS

N

CANADA

U S A

New York

Washington

Soviet convoy stopped here

Gulf of Mexico

Quarantine line

MEXICO

Havana   Miami

CUBA

ATLANTIC

OCEAN

0 km 1000

0 miles 500

S O U T H
A M E R I C A

The island of Cuba lies close to the USA. The Americans imposed a 'quarantine line' 500 miles off Cuba through which Soviet ships were not allowed to pass.

ON THE VERGE OF WAR

Oct 24, Washington "I sat across from the President. This was the moment we had prepared for, which we hoped would never come. The danger and concern that we all felt hung like a cloud over us all . . . These few minutes were the time of greatest worry by the President. His hand went up to his face and covered his mouth and he closed his fist. His eyes were tense, almost gray, and we just stared at each other across the table. Was the world on the brink of a holocaust and had we done something wrong? . . . We had come to the edge of a final decision, and the President agreed. I felt we were on the edge of a precipice and it was as if there were no way off."

(Robert Kennedy quoted in *Robert Kennedy and his times*, Arthur Schlesinger Jun., Andre Deutsch 1978)

THREAT OF NUCLEAR WAR LIFTED

Oct 28, Washington The risk of a nuclear war over Cuba appears to have gone. The Americans and the Russians have both backed down. The Soviets have undertaken to destroy their Cuban launch pads and ship all missiles on the island back to Russia. In return the Americans have pledged not to attack Cuba and will lift the blockade immediately.

AFRICAN LEADER JAILED

Nov 7, Pretoria, South Africa A court in Pretoria has sentenced Nelson Mandela to five years in jail. He was found guilty of planning a national strike and of encouraging violent rebellion by the non-white population against the white Government of South Africa. Mr. Mandela's imprisonment may silence his voice for a while but it will make him a hero to the black people of his country.

In Alabama, fireman and police train hoses on 2000 black demonstrators for civil rights. The crowd held a march and prayer meeting. Some 400 police and 250 highway patrolmen guarded the city.

LESSONS OF THE CRISIS

Oct 29, Washington The Russians and Americans have been badly shaken by the Cuban crisis. Both realize that a single unwise move might have pitched the whole world into nuclear war. They are working out new and better ways of talking to each other if dangerous disagreements arise in future.

RACE RIOTS AT US COLLEGE

Oct 1, Oxford, Mississippi Only white students are allowed to study at universities in America's southern states. Blacks are not admitted. Yesterday a black man, James Meredith, arrived at the local college and signed on as a student. Thousands of angry whites stormed the college buildings and demanded that the authorities should cancel Meredith's entry. A force of 750 federal marshals failed to restore order. Three people died and over fifty were injured in the fighting. Today President Kennedy sent in a larger group of marshals to escort Meredith to his classes. The whites continued to protest and a further 200 have been arrested. Rioting has spread to other cities.

NEWS IN BRIEF . . .

A BRIGHTER BRITISH SUNDAY

Feb 4, London A new venture in British newspaper publishing is launched today. The *Sunday Times* appears in two parts. The familiar black-and-white newspaper is joined by a separate magazine-type supplement in full colour. Few think it will last.

FIRST AMERICAN IN SPACE

Feb 20, Cape Canaveral The Americans have put a man into space. John Glenn was picked up from the sea off Puerto Rico this afternoon at the end of a flight which had taken him three times round the earth. The space race between the USA and the USSR is gaining pace!

John Glenn preparing for the launch

SMOG KILLS 60 IN LONDON

Dec 6, London Smog has claimed 60 victims in London in the past three days. The lethal mixture of smoke and fog is likely to blanket the capital for another 24 hours, say the forecasters.

COVENTRY'S CATHEDRAL RISES AGAIN

May 25, Coventry Twenty years ago last November, German bombers laid waste large areas of the city of Coventry and destroyed the cathedral. Today, Coventry's new cathedral was consecrated. It stands on the ruins of the old building and has been designed and decorated by some of Britain's finest architects and artists.

Interior view of Coventry Cathedral

BRILLIANT BRAZIL KEEPS CUP

June 17, Santiago, Chile The Brazilians remain the leaders in world soccer. They beat the Czechs here today 3–1 and retain the World Cup they won four years ago.

WORLD'S FIRST HOVERCRAFT SERVICE

July 20, Rhyl, Wales The world's first public hovercraft service began today. Regular trips across the River Dee will link Rhyl in North Wales with Wallasey in Cheshire. The hovercraft carries 24 passengers, at 110 kph (69 mph). Hovercraft are the invention of British engineer Christopher Cockerell.

MARILYN MONROE FOUND DEAD

Aug 5, Hollywood The film actress Marilyn Monroe was found dead early today in her Hollywood home. An empty bottle of sleeping tablets lay nearby. Marilyn Monroe was enormously successful as an actress but a deeply troubled person in her private life. Her three marriages broke up and in June this year she was sacked by her studio for repeatedly failing to arrive for work. It seems that her unhappiness has finally caused her to take her own life. She was only 36.

ART CRITICS SQUABBLE

Nov, New York Is this rubbish or is this art? Andy Warhol's careful painting of a can of soup, now on show at a smart New York gallery, has art critics in a dither. Warhol is one of the new generation of American painters and sculptors working in an inventive new style known as Pop Art.

Big Campbell's Soup Can, 19¢ by Andy Warhol

1963

DEATH OF A PRESIDENT
KENNEDY SHOT DEAD

Nov 22, Dallas, Texas President Kennedy is dead. He was shot while riding in an open car through the streets of Dallas to a political meeting. His wife Jackie was at his side but escaped injury. John Connally, the Governor of Texas, was travelling in the same car and is seriously wounded.

A Dallas policeman was shot shortly after the President was killed. An ex-US marine named Oswald has been charged with the policeman's murder. Vice-President Lyndon B. Johnson has been sworn in as President of the United States. Kennedy's widow, Jackie, shocked and dazed, stood at Johnson's shoulder as he took the oath.

OSWALD CHARGED WITH KENNEDY'S DEATH

Nov 22, Dallas Lee Harvey Oswald has been charged with the murder of President Kennedy.

TV MILLIONS SEE OSWALD SHOT

Nov 24, Dallas Lee Harvey Oswald, the man accused of killing America's president, himself lies dead. Oswald, under police guard, was being transferred to the county gaol. A bystander stepped forward, rammed a revolver into Oswald's ribs and pulled the trigger. Oswald died instantly. The entire episode was watched by TV viewers throughout North America.

President Kennedy in his motorcade cruises through Dallas minutes before the assassination.

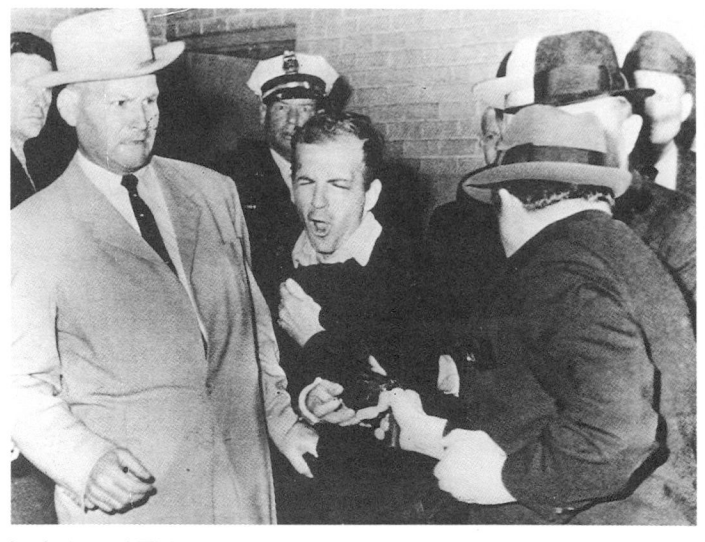

In front of TV cameras, Jack Ruby shoots Lee Harvey Oswald.

THE WORLD MOURNS KENNEDY

Nov 25, Washington Representatives from 93 nations have joined the American people in mourning the death of President Kennedy. Thousands of people, many in tears, lined Washington's hushed streets as the murdered President's body was taken to be buried in Arlington national cemetery.

OSWALD'S MURDERER ACCUSED

Nov 26, Dallas Jack Ruby, a local nightclub owner, has been accused of Oswald's murder. Mystery surrounds both that killing and the shooting of the President. If Oswald killed Kennedy, why did he do it? What made Ruby kill Oswald? Neither murderer seems to have had a clear motive.

THIEVES' MILLION POUND HAUL

Aug 8, Cheddington, England In a well-planned robbery near this small Buckinghamshire village, a gang of thieves has made off with more than a million pounds. At 3.10 a.m., a train carrying a load of worn bank-notes, on their way to be destroyed, was halted by a stop signal on the railway line nearby. The robbers waiting by the track broke into the train, coshed the driver and handcuffed the fireman. They loaded 120 mailbags full of notes onto a lorry and drove off. The police have begun a nation-wide search for the criminals.

JUDGE TO INVESTIGATE ASSASSINATION

Nov 29, Washington President Johnson has set up a Commission to investigate the shooting of President Kennedy. America's most respected judge, Earl Warren, is to head the enquiry.

Police are searching all over the country for the thieves who drove the train to this bridge. From here, mailbags were loaded onto a waiting lorry.

NEWS IN BRIEF . . .

LOW LIFE IN HIGH PLACES

Aug 7, London   For the past two months British headlines have been dominated by a scandal. It involves a Cabinet minister, a Russian diplomat, a West End doctor, a millionaire or two, assorted politicians and a number of exceedingly pretty girls. The War Minister John Profumo, the central figure in the affair, has resigned. The scandal has rocked the government. An eminent judge has been appointed to question those involved and to write a report on the whole wretched business.

John Profumo, former minister

DEATH OF POPE JOHN

June 3, Rome   Pope John XXIII, the best-loved pope of modern times, has died. Pope John was plain-spoken and warm-hearted. People felt he cared. He was a reforming pope, and in his brief four-year reign strove to bring the Christian churches of the world closer together.

BRITISH RAILWAYS FACE HUGE CUTS

March 27, London   A Government committee under Dr. Richard Beeching has been looking at better and cheaper ways of running Britain's railways. It has now finished its work. In his report, Dr. Beeching recommends closing over 2000 stations, and says that a quarter of the railway track should be closed. Outlying parts of the British Isles, and villages and small towns in the countryside, would lose their rail links. There is bound to be fierce opposition from the areas worst affected. Members of Parliament representing them will try to have the report rejected when it comes before Parliament later this year.

CREDIT CARDS COME TO BRITAIN

Sept 10, Britain   This month, America's most popular credit card, American Express, is launched in Britain. But the little plastic card won't be available to just anybody. People must earn at least £2000 a year in order to have one.

BEATLES STAR IN ROYAL SHOW

Nov 5, London   What a year it has been for the Beatles! In April, the lads from Liverpool had their first No. 1 hit. Their latest single, 'I wanna hold your hand', sold a million copies within three days of its release. Last night's appearance at the Royal Variety Performance has crowned the Beatles' year of triumph.

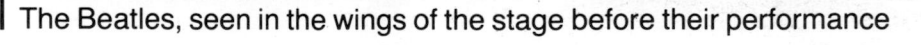

The Beatles, seen in the wings of the stage before their performance

1964

WAR IN VIETNAM
US FIGHTS COMMUNISM IN S.E. ASIA

June 20, Washington The anxiety of the American government grows as the Communists strengthen their hold on south-east Asia. Vietnam is most at risk. The country is divided in two. Red China and the Soviet Union support North Vietnam while South Vietnam is backed by the United States. Communist guerrillas, known as the Vietcong, trained and armed by the North Vietnamese, have overrun large areas of the South. Groups of specially-trained US military personnel are serving alongside the South Vietnamese forces in a campaign to hunt them down. So far these US troops and their allies have had little success. The Vietcong control most of the South outside the main cities.

A South Vietnamese woman abandons her burning village.

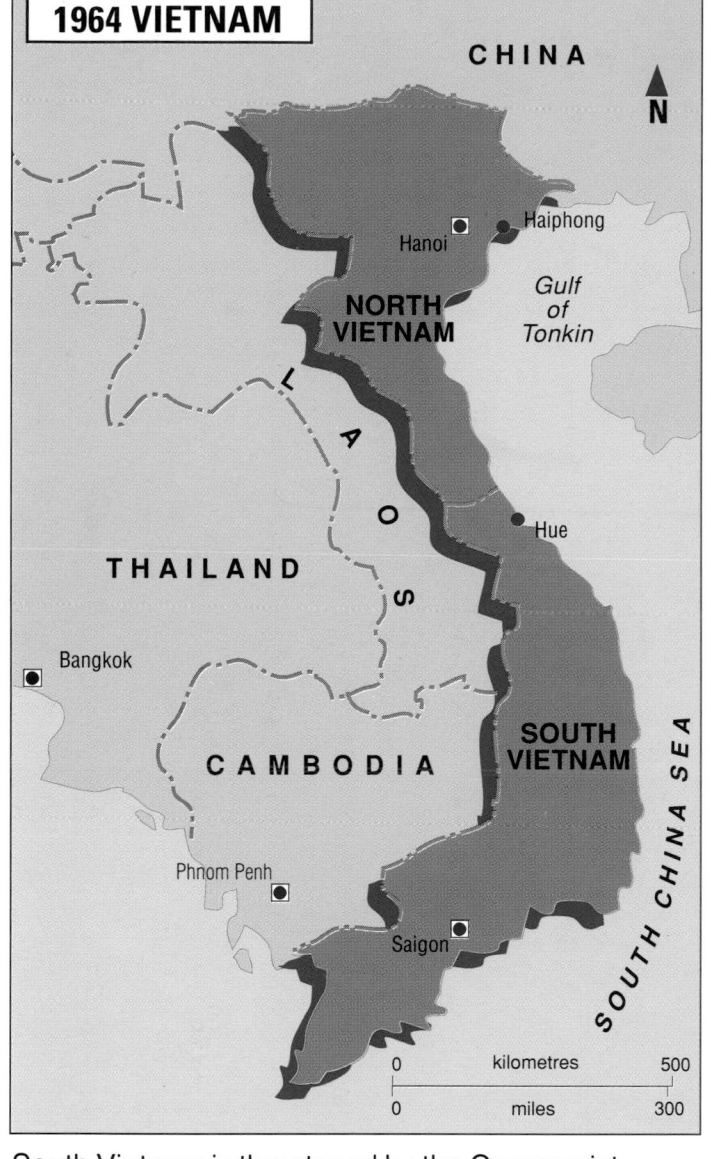

1964 VIETNAM

CHINA

Hanoi
Haiphong

NORTH VIETNAM

Gulf of Tonkin

LAOS

THAILAND

Hue

Bangkok

CAMBODIA

SOUTH VIETNAM

Phnom Penh

Saigon

SOUTH CHINA SEA

| 0 | kilometres | 500 |
| 0 | miles | 300 |

South Vietnam is threatened by the Communist North.

US AIRCRAFT BOMB NORTH VIETNAM

Aug 5, Gulf of Tonkin   North Vietnamese torpedo boats have fired on ships of the US Seventh Fleet patrolling the Gulf of Tonkin. US aircraft have hit back by bombing naval bases on shore.

JOHNSON WINS US ELECTION

Nov 3, Washington   Lyndon Johnson stays in the White House. He beat his opponent Barry Goldwater in a landslide victory. Johnson promises civil rights at home in America and continued backing for the South Vietnamese.

PALESTINE ISSUE UNITES ARABS

May 31, Cairo   Arab leaders meeting in Cairo have set up an organization to unite the different groups of Palestinian refugees. The new body is to be called The Palestine Liberation Organization. Saudi Arabia has promised to provide the PLO with the money it will need to carry on the fight against the Israelis. The Arabs have named 1970 as the provisional date for the war against Israel to liberate Palestine.

KHRUSHCHEV TOPPLED

Oct 15, Moscow   A plot hatched by his enemies in the Kremlin has brought down the soviet leader Nikita Khrushchev. Khrushchev, at 70, has been replaced as party leader by Leonid Brezhnev and as Prime Minister by Alexei Kosygin.

Nikita Khrushchev (left) on a visit to Sweden, with King Gustav

Lyndon Johnson during his presidential campaign

TURKEY AND GREECE HALT CYPRUS WAR

Aug 10, New York The Turks and the Greeks have accepted the United Nations terms for a cease-fire in Cyprus. This agreement ends, for the time being, the fighting between the Greek and Turkish communities who both live on the island. The peace is unlikely to last, for the hatred between Greeks and Turks is as bitter as ever. Furthermore, the Greeks disagree among themselves. Many regard their leader, Archbishop Makarios, as a traitor for agreeing to the UN plan. There have already been several attempts to kill him.

The Cypriot president, Archbishop Makarios, inspects Greek Cypriot troops in Nicosia.

NEWS IN BRIEF . . .

CLAY WINS WORLD HEAVYWEIGHT TITLE

Feb 25, Miami Beach Cassius Clay has proved his critics wrong by winning tonight's world title bout against Sonny Liston in seven rounds. Clay boasts "I am the greatest!" and he is without doubt a superb boxer. He has other talents. He has a record in the pop charts and can hold his own with any chat-show presenter. In the ring or out of it, Cassius Clay is a vibrant and memorable personality.

Cassius Clay stands over the fallen Sonny Liston during the first minute of their fight.

BEATLEMANIA USA

Feb 29, New York Seventy million Americans watched the Beatles on the Ed Sullivan television show. The appearance was the summit of their recent American tour. Frenzied crowds have packed every performance the Beatles have given in the States.

DEATH OF INDIA'S NEHRU

May 28, New Delhi Jawaharlal Nehru, India's Prime Minister, died suddenly yesterday of a heart attack. Mr. Nehru will be mourned by millions of Indians and by his admirers throughout the world. He was a leader in the struggle for India's freedom and has guided the country since independence was achieved in 1947. World leaders are gathering in New Delhi for the dead premier's cremation which will take place tomorrow. His ashes will be cast into the water where the Rivers Ganges and Jumna meet.

THE TOKYO OLYMPICS

Oct 24, Tokyo Soviet athletes top the winners' list at the Tokyo Olympics with 96 medals. The United States follows with 90. Altogether, 41 of the competing nations won a medal of some kind. Peter Snell, of New Zealand, confirmed that he is a truly great middle-distance runner by winning both the 800 and 1500 metres. The host nation Japan did well in its traditional events, gymnastics, judo and wrestling. Mary Rand and Lynn Davies recorded a unique double for Britain by winning between them the women's and the men's long jump event.

LIFE SENTENCE FOR MANDELA

June 14, Pretoria Nelson Mandela has been sentenced to life imprisonment for sabotage and for plotting against the white government of South Africa.

MARTIN LUTHER KING HONOURED

Oct 24, Oslo The Nobel Peace Prize for 1964 has gone to Dr. Martin Luther King, leader of the equal rights campaign for black people in America.

CHINA'S ATOM BOMB

Oct 16, Peking The Chinese exploded their first atom bomb today at a test site in Sinkiang. The United States, the USSR, Britain and France have the bomb. China now becomes the fifth member of the world nuclear club. The Chinese claim that they built the bomb to protect themselves against the United States. They accuse the Americans of attempting to plunge the world into nuclear war.

Britain's Mary Rand (centre), gold medal winner of the women's long jump

1965

THE CIVIL RIGHTS BATTLE
VIOLENCE IN ALABAMA

March 10, Selma, Alabama The white population of this small town in America's Deep South are up in arms. They are protesting because regulations that prevented black people from voting in elections have been made illegal. Two days ago, Selma police armed with clubs and whips broke up a protest march of local blacks. The marchers were not violent, and there was no excuse for the police to attack them.

Today, there is news of a white clergyman beaten almost to death by other whites as he left a church used by black people. Other unprovoked attacks by whites on black people, and on whites who support them, are reported from several places in the southern American states.

State troopers attack negro John Lewis at Selma, Alabama. Mr. Lewis was later admitted to hospital.

CIVIL RIGHTS MARCH

March 25, Montgomery, Alabama A crowd of 25,000 demonstrators massed today in Alabama's capital to deliver a civil rights petition to State Governor Wallace. The presentation came at the end of an 80 km (50 mile) march from Selma, headed by civil rights leader Dr. Martin Luther King. Several well-known sympathizers were there to greet the marchers: singers Joan Baez and Harry Belafonte, entertainer Sammy Davis Jun., novelist James Baldwin and conductor Leonard Bernstein. Critics of Dr. King say that he is turning the civil rights movement into a branch of show business.

Dr. Martin Luther King arrives at the Alabama State Capitol to present his petition.

VICTORY FOR CIVIL RIGHTS

Aug 6, Washington The Voting Rights Act is now law. The Act, signed by President Johnson in the presence of civil rights leaders, will give the vote to hundreds of thousands of black people in America's southern states. The long supremacy of the whites in the South may be about to end.

RACE HATRED EXPLODES

Aug 17, Watts, Los Angeles Five days of savage rioting have devastated this drab suburb of Los Angeles. Police brutality against local blacks brought out crowds of protesters who turned on the police, attacked whites and destroyed property. The orgy of burning, looting and violence ended only after 18,000 National Guardsmen had been drafted in to suppress it. A commission is to be set up to enquire into the causes of the riots. People who know Watts say that the misery and resentment of poverty and high unemployment caused the recent outburst.

WHITE RHODESIANS DEFY BRITAIN

Nov 11, Salisbury The quarrel between Britain and the whites who govern Rhodesia has come to a head. In a broadcast today, Ian Smith, Prime Minister of this colony in southern Africa, has declared Rhodesia independent of Britain. His aim is to prevent Britain from organizing an election in which, for the first time in Rhodesia, blacks would be able to vote. Equal voting rights for blacks and whites would end white rule in the colony, Smith fears, and put a black govenment in power.

The Rhodesian leader Ian Smith in London for crucial talks

TRADE BLOCKADE OF RHODESIA

Nov 16, London Britain will not use force to put down Ian Smith's rebellion. The Government intends to use peaceful means of persuasion. It will block trade with Rhodesia and so 'bring the rebels to their senses' by making it impossible for them to run the country. Parliament in London is rushing through the laws necessary to halt trade with Ian Smith's illegal regime.

US TROOPS POUR INTO VIETNAM

Dec 31, Washington Back in July, President Johnson pledged that in Vietnam the Americans would not surrender nor retreat. Increasing numbers of young Americans are beng sucked into the war in Indo-China to back his promise. US troops serving in Vietnam now number 184,000. The monthly call-up has risen from 17,000 to 35,000 in order to support the war effort.

NEWS IN BRIEF . . .

WORLD'S FAREWELL TO CHURCHILL
Jan 30, London Winston Churchill died six days ago. He was by turns soldier, war reporter, novelist, historian, painter, politician and world statesman. He has been honoured in a funeral fit for a king. Leading figures of 110 nations came to London to pay their respects. After the service in St. Paul's Cathedral, Churchill's body was taken for burial in the churchyard at Bladon in Oxfordshire. It is close by the palace of Blenheim where he was born 90 years ago.

SHORT SKIRTS RAISE PROBLEMS
Sept, London Paris invented the mini-skirt, but it is London dress-designer Mary Quant who has made it popular. Rising hemlines are causing problems, particularly at school. To their pupils' fury, many schools insist that a school uniform skirt should be long enough to touch the ground when the girl kneels down. On the other hand, boys are in trouble if their hair is too long. Hair 'above the collar' is the general regulation.

Sailors flank Churchill's coffin in the huge funeral procession.

BEATLES' MBE OFFENDS
June 20, London Not everybody is pleased that the Beatles have been made MBEs in the Queen's Birthday Honours. The quality newspapers complain that the award to a group of pop music entertainers lowers the value of the honours system, and makes it ridiculous. Two holders of the award have even sent their medals back in protest.

BRITAIN ENDS HANGING
Nov 9, London From today, no one found guilty of murder in Britain can be executed.

TV CIGARETTE ADVERTS BANNED
Aug 1, London The Government has at last heeded the warning on smoking and lung cancer. Now there will be no more cigarette advertising on British TV.

1966

CHAIRMAN MAO'S NEW REVOLUTION

Oct 30, Peking The chairman of the Chinese Communist party, Mao Tse-tung, is using the young people of China to bring about a 'cultural revolution'. He believes that violent changes are necessary to make China into an ideal Communist state. Urged on by Mao in his speeches and writings, millions of students have left their studies. They dress in army uniforms and wear red armbands. Mao calls them his Red Guards.

RED GUARDS TERRORIZE CHINA

Nov 19, Peking China is in turmoil. Mobs of teenage Red Guards have attacked and, in some cases, killed their teachers. People who seem to be too well-off to be true Communists are taken from their homes and forced to work on farms or in factories. Ancient temples have been destroyed and precious works of art smashed. Chairman Mao teaches that such things are harmful or set a bad example in modern China.

The Chinese Cultural Revolution is felt even in Britain. These Chinese demonstrators are in London.

MAJOR OFFENSIVE IN VIETNAM

Jan 9, Saigon   The Americans are taking over this jungle war. Until now, US troops have only gone into action at the request of the South Vietnamese. Yesterday, in the heaviest fighting since war started, the US Command ignored their allies and made an all-American attack on the Vietcong.

NEHRU'S DAUGHTER TO LEAD INDIA

Jan 19, New Delhi   Large crowds gathered outside Parliament House to cheer Indira Gandhi when it became known that she had been elected to lead India's government. Mrs. Gandhi is the daughter of Pandit Nehru, the first Prime Minister of independent India. In her first speech, the new Prime Minister promised to follow her father's policy of peace toward all nations.

GROWING US FORCE IN VIETNAM

Dec 31, Saigon   Total American strength in South Vietnam has risen to 385,000 troops.

Mrs. Gandhi is sworn in as Prime Minister.

NEWS IN BRIEF . . .

AUSSIES JOIN IN VIETNAM WAR

April 20, Saigon   The Australian government is sending troops to Vietnam to join the Americans in the fight against the Communists. The first party flew in to Vietnam this morning.

HUGE NORTH SEA GAS FINDS

Dec 12, London   There is enough natural gas in the rocks under the North Sea to supply all of Britain's needs for many years. The latest gas strike announced today comes at the end of a year of promising discoveries. Hopes are rising that oil as well as gas lies buried off Britain's shores.

Half-way through his trip round the world, Francis Chichester sails alone into Sydney harbour, Australia.

Mr. Wilson (centre) with his senior ministers: Ray Gunter, George Brown, Walter Padley, Barbara Castle and Len Williams

LABOUR TRIUMPHS IN UK ELECTIONS

April 1, London British voters have put Harold Wilson and the Labour Party back in power with a majority of 96 MPs. This margin should mean a more settled period of government. For the past 18 months Labour has struggled on with a tiny majority of just four seats.

ENGLAND WIN WORLD CUP

July 30, London The English invented football but it has taken them over 100 years to win the game's highest honour, the World Cup. The trophy became theirs this afternoon, at Wembley Stadium, after beating West Germany 4–2 in the final.

Captain Bobby Moore holds aloft the World Cup after England's victory.

ASSASSIN KNIFES PREMIER

Sept 6, Cape Town, South Africa Dr. Hendrik Verwoerd, Prime Minister of South Africa, has been murdered in the House of Assembly. He was stabbed four times and died instantly. Other Government ministers overpowered the assassin. The killer is a white man named Dimitri Tsafendas. He seems to have borne a grudge against the Prime Minister. Fellow workers say he blamed the Government for doing too little to help poor whites in South Africa.

Dr. Verwoerd, South African premier

WELSH SCHOOL ENGULFED

Oct 27, Aberfan Six days ago, over 130 people died in this small Welsh village; 116 of them were children. They were killed as a coal tip overlooking the village slid down the hillside and swallowed up the village school. The tip was made of thousands of tons of wet mud and rock. There were scenes of heart-rending grief as 82 of the victims were buried today. The Government has ordered a high-level inquiry into the cause of the disaster.

1967

MIDDLE EAST TENSION GROWS

April 30, Damascus, Syria The Middle East is edging towards conflict. Palestinian Al-Fatah guerrillas make daily raids into Israel from bases in Jordan and Syria. Syrian guns on the Golan Heights regularly shell Israeli settlements on the plains below. Israeli aircraft have struck back at the Syrian gun positions. Across Israel's southern border, President Nasser of Egypt declares he is preparing his country for war.

MIDDLE EAST CRISIS DEEPENS

May 23, Cairo, Egypt Egypt has closed the Straits of Tiran to Israeli ships, stopping Israel's only outlet to the Indian Ocean. The blockade comes after the withdrawal of United Nations' troops from Sinai at Egypt's request. This UN peace-keeping force has kept the Israelis and Egyptians apart for the past ten years. Egypt is threatening Israel by massing 100,000 troops and 1000 tanks in Sinai, close to the Israeli border.

A column of Israeli soldiers on the march in Israel to confront Arab forces

LIGHTNING STRIKE ON ARAB AIR POWER

June 6, Tel Aviv, Israel   At breakfast time yesterday, Israeli aircraft appeared over Egypt's main airfields. From intelligence reports the Israelis knew that most Egyptian aircraft would be grounded at that time of day. Within hours, the Egyptian airforce had been destroyed. In the afternoon, Israeli planes struck at airfields in Jordan, Syria and Iraq. The result there was the same. By yesterday evening, the Arab airforces had ceased to exist. On the ground, Israeli armoured columns have attacked and broken through Egyptian positions in Sinai.

EGYPT AND JORDAN ACCEPT CEASEFIRE

June 7, Tel Aviv   Israeli troops have reached the Suez Canal and now occupy the entire Sinai peninsula. During the battle, hundreds of Egyptian tanks and vehicles jammed in the Mitla Pass were destroyed as they attempted to retreat westward. On the eastern front, the Israelis have driven the Jordanians out of East Jerusalem and from the West Bank area of Palestine. Israel, Egypt and Jordan have accepted the ceasefire put forward by the United Nations. Fighting between them has ended. The war with Syria in the Golan Heights goes on.

MIDDLE EAST FIGHTING ENDS

June 10, Tel Aviv   The Israelis have driven the Syrians from the Golan Heights and Syria has agreed to the UN ceasefire. Israel's victory is complete. In this six-day war, her armies have captured East Jerusalem, the West Bank, the Sinai Peninsula and the Golan Heights. Israel has increased its territory size by more than 200 per cent. Over 100,000 Arabs left their homes in the fighting and are now refugees. The Israeli army leader, General Moshe Dayan, has been acclaimed a national hero. Yet long-term peace in the Middle East is as far off as ever. The Israelis may feel safer behind their new borders, but the Arabs will never rest until they have regained their lost lands and set up an Arab state of Palestine.

ARMY COLONELS SEIZE GREECE

April 21, Athens   A group of right-wing army officers, called the 'junta' of colonels, today seized power from the democratic government. The junta is led by Colonel Georges Papadopoulos, in the name of the Greek King. The democratic leader, Georges Papandreou, is under arrest.

DE GAULLE SAYS "NON"

May 16, Paris   Britain's latest application to join the European Common Market is certain to be turned down. France's President de Gaulle is against it. He maintains that the British are attached too closely to the Americans to be allowed into the European Community.

SIR FRANCIS COMES HOME

May 28, Plymouth, England   119 days after setting out from Plymouth to sail round the world single-handed, 65-year-old Francis Chichester has come home. He returns as Sir Francis. In January 1966, the Queen conferred a knighthood on him when he was half-way on his 49,000 km (30,000 miles) voyage, at Sydney. The Queen will dub him with Sir Francis Drake's sword at Greenwich.

NIGERIA BREAKS UP

May 30, Enugu, Nigeria   The Ibo people in eastern Nigeria have broken away from the rest of the country and set up an independent state they call Biafra. The Ibo leader Colonel Ojukwu accuses the other Nigerian peoples of deliberate attempts to wipe out the Ibos. A separate state is the Ibo's only chance of survival, he says.

WAR IN BIAFRA

July 31, Enugu   Nigeria is now at war with the break-away state of Biafra. The main fighting is in the north, as Federal Nigerian troops try to advance towards the Biafran capital here in Enugu.

NO END TO VIETNAM WAR

Nov 21, Saigon, South Vietnam American aircraft have made the heaviest raids of the war so far on North Vietnam. Apart from military damage, many civilians have been killed in the attacks. At home in the United States, opposition to the war is growing. There are now over 450,000 Americans serving in Vietnam.

An anti-war demonstration is broken up by police.

WITH THE VIETCONG

Dec 10, near Hanoi "Through the daylight hours nothing moves on the roads of North Vietnam, not a car nor a truck. It must look from the air as though the country had no wheeled transport at all. That, of course, is the idea, it is the roads and bridges that are being bombed; it is no longer safe after sunrise to be anywhere near either. . .

When the sun goes down everything starts to move. . . At dusk the roads become alive. The engines are started and the convoys grind away through the darkness behind the pinpoints of masked headlamps. There are miles of them, heavy Russian-built trucks, anti-aircraft batteries, all deeply buried under piles of branches and leaves. . . North Vietnam by day is abandoned; by night it thuds and grinds with movement. It is a fatiguing routine: working by day and moving by night."

(James Cameron, from *What a way to own the tribe*, Macmillan 1968)

NEWS IN BRIEF . . .

OIL DEVASTATES CORNISH BEACHES

April 2, Penzance, England A fortnight ago, the huge oil tanker *Torrey Canyon* ran aground on the Seven Stones Reef off the Cornish coast. The reef tore the ship open and 100,000 tons of oil have since spilled into the sea. The foul, stinking ooze is washing ashore on 150 km (90 miles) of the coastline. Bird, fish and plant life is devastated.

The wreck of the oil tanker *Torrey Canyon*. Treatment with detergents has failed to prevent oil reaching Cornish beaches.

The first public showing of Concorde

CONCORDE UNVEILED

Dec 11, Toulouse, France   The public has had its first glimpse of the Concorde. This morning test model 001, being built by the French at Toulouse, was rolled out on to the tarmac. The French and British aircraft industries are working together to develop and build the Concorde. It will be the world's first supersonic passenger aircraft and is a fine example of Anglo-French co-operation.

THE SUMMER OF LOVE

Sept 1, London Last January, thousands of young Americans gathered in San Francisco's Golden Gate Park to chant mystic Indian verses, smoke pot and sway to the rhythm of acid rock bands. They called it the San Francisco 'Be-In'. Now the Be-In has come to Britain. Last week the Duke of Bedford opened the grounds of his stately home, Woburn Abbey, for a 'Festival of Love'. Young people from all over Britain, some with small children, flocked to it. They came in clothes of all colours, draped with beads and decked in flowers and necklaces of small silver bells. They spent three happy days at Woburn; there was no violence and no one was hurt. Those who forecast a weekend of rioting have been proved wrong.

MAN GIVEN NEW HEART

Dec 3, Cape Town, South Africa Surgeon Christiaan Barnard has carried out the first successful transplant of a human heart. The patient is doing well after the operation. According to Dr. Barnard, the operation was straightforward but he says that no one knows yet whether the patient's body will accept the new heart.

Dr. Christiaan Barnard, the surgeon

CAMPBELL DIES IN SPEED TRAGEDY

Jan 4, Coniston Water, England Donald Campbell perished today in an attempt to beat the world water-speed record. As it raced across Coniston Water at 480 kph (300 mph), Campbell's speedboat *Bluebird* leapt into the air and cartwheeled before plunging below the surface.

1968

AMERICA'S RACIAL VIOLENCE
SNIPER KILLS MARTIN LUTHER KING

April 4, Memphis, USA The American Civil Rights leader Dr. Martin Luther King has been shot dead. He was talking to friends on their motel balcony when the bullet, fired from a distance, struck him. The killer escaped.

THOUSANDS MOURN MARTIN LUTHER KING

April 9, Atlanta, USA Dr. Martin Luther King has had a hero's burial. Over 150,000 people crowded into Atlanta for his funeral. The coffin passed through the grieving multitude, lying on a plain wooden farm cart drawn by two mules. At the graveside, a recording of the dead man's last sermon was played as his own funeral oration.

Friends join hands at the funeral in Atlanta, Georgia, of Dr. Martin Luther King.

AMERICA BURNS AFTER KING'S MURDER

April 11, Washington Martin Luther King's murder has stirred up widespread violence. Across America, mobs of black people ran wild when they heard that their leader had been shot. Over 100 cities felt the fury of the rioters. Here in the capital, tanks and armoured cars came out to patrol the streets, and buildings were set ablaze within sight of the White House, the President's home.

AFTER THE VIOLENCE

Dec 17, Washington Martin Luther King did not die in vain. Thanks to him and to those he led, the laws which denied rights to black Americans have been swept away. But racial prejudice in America is far from over, and racial violence will return. The struggle that Martin King led for full equality for all Americans must go on.

BOBBY KENNEDY SHOT DEAD

June 6, Los Angeles, USA A 20-hour fight to save the life of Senator Bobby Kennedy has failed. Kennedy had just delivered a speech accepting nomination for president when he was shot at point-blank range. The killer is a young Palestinian. He shouted "I did it for my country!" as Kennedy fell, mortally wounded. It is believed that Kennedy's support for Israel made him a target for supporters of the Palestinian cause in the Middle East.

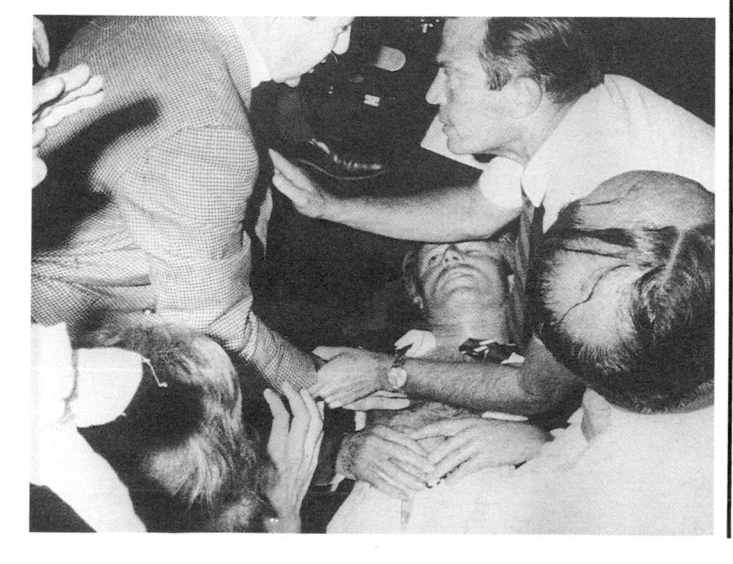

REBELS LOSING NIGERIAN WAR

May 8, Lagos, Nigeria Nigerian troops have captured Port Harcourt and now occupy most of the main centres of population in the breakaway state of Biafra. However, the Biafran rebels still control large areas around the cities. They are determined to continue to fight even though they can have no hope of winning the war.

A Biafran soldier awaits advancing Nigerian forces.

NIXON TO BE NEXT PRESIDENT

Nov 6, Washington The Republican candidate Richard Nixon has been elected President of the United States. This was Nixon's second attempt to enter the White House. In the election eight years ago he was narrowly defeated by John F. Kennedy. The new president inherits immense problems: the global Cold War between capitalism and Communism, the war in Vietnam and continuing violence in America's towns and cities.

THE PRAGUE SPRING

THE CZECHS EDGE TOWARDS FREEDOM

March 13, Prague Czechoslovakia has been in the grip of the Soviet Union since 1945 when World War II ended. Since then, the Czechs have endured the same harsh laws as the people of the other Communist countries of Eastern Europe. But now the government of Alexander Dubcek has ended censorship. From today, newspapers in Czechoslovakia are free to print the news as they see it. Dubcek came to power in January. Thanks to his reforms this 'Prague Spring', there is already more liberty in Czechoslovakia than in any other country on the Soviet side of the Iron Curtain.

Mr. Alexander Dubcek surrounded by his supporters

SOVIET TANKS ROLL INTO PRAGUE TO CRUSH CZECH LIBERTY

Aug 22, Prague Soviet troops and tanks occupy Prague. Alexander Dubcek and his senior ministers have been arrested. Communist Party officials who opposed the Dubcek reforms have replaced them and Czechoslovakia is back under Soviet control. The Czech people are in despair, for they are powerless to resist the Russian invasion. Soviet newspapers claim that the Czechs are grateful to the Russian troops for putting an end to the Dubcek regime.

Soviet tanks entering Prague on the first day of the invasion of Czechoslovakia

NEWS IN BRIEF . . .

FIRST SPACE MAN KILLED

March 27, Moscow Yuri Gagarin, the first man into space, is dead. He was killed today when the aircraft he was piloting crashed, 50 km (31 miles) from Moscow.

ZEPPELIN OVER AMERICA

Dec 15, New York Britain has provided the biggest new rock music act of the year in the USA. Led Zeppelin, a group put together by guitarist Jimmy Page, has stunned America with its amazingly powerful sound. Another group, Cream, isn't far behind. The local reply to the British invasion hasn't been slow in coming. Blue Cheer, Iron Butterfly and Spirit lead the bands in America's charts.

ASTRONAUTS CIRCLE THE MOON

Dec 27, Cape Kennedy, USA A spacecraft carrying three astronauts splashed down into the Pacific today after a six-day mission which took it ten times round the moon. US space officials are delighted with the success of this mission. Their next target is the moon itself.

Athletes Tommie Smith and John Carlos give the Black Power salute.

BLACK POWER AT MEXICO OLYMPICS

Oct 27, Mexico City Politics rather than athletics have been the main feature of these games. Two black American athletes, standing on the victors' rostrum, raised a black-gloved fist in a defiant Black Power salute under the American national flag while the American national anthem was being played. Their protest was watched by millions of television viewers world-wide. The two runners were making a personal sacrifice; they were expelled from the American team and sent home in disgrace.

1969

MEN ON THE MOON
THE MOON FLIGHT BEGINS

July 16, Kennedy Space Center, USA At 9.32 a.m. this morning, *Apollo 11* took off for the moon. Three thousand reporters were at the site, and the million sightseers jammed the roads around the Kennedy Space Center. They cheered and prayed as the 111 m-high (364 ft) Saturn rocket rose from its launch pad and headed up into the sky over the Atlantic. Around the world, 600 million television viewers watched the lift-off. The three astronauts, Neil Armstrong, 'Buzz' Aldrin and Michael Collins, are now on course for a moon landing four days from now. The world watches and waits.

"WE HAVE NO COMPLAINTS"

July 19, Houston Space Center Everything has gone according to plan. The Saturn rocket boosted the command module Columbia and the mooncraft Eagle to a speed of 40,000 kph (24,800 mph) before falling away and burning up in the earth's atmosphere. The crew are pleased with the flight so far. "It was beautiful. We have no complaints," said Neil Armstrong, the *Apollo 11* commander, during one of yesterday's television transmissions from Columbia as it hurtled on its path towards the moon.

Apollo 11 lifts off at Kennedy Space Center, USA. Crew members are Neil Armstrong, Michael Collins and Edwin 'Buzz' Aldrin. Armstrong and Aldrin are due to land on the moon on July 20.

The lunar module approaches the surface of the moon.

THE EAGLE HAS LANDED

July 21, Houston Space Center Cameras on board the mooncraft beamed back to earth pictures of the final moments of Eagle's descent to the dusty surface of the moon. At 3.17 p.m. Houston time yesterday, a sigh of relief went up around the world as Neil Armstrong guided the Eagle the last few metres down to a safe landing. A minute later he made his historic report back to earth, "The Eagle has landed". Four hours later, Armstrong and Aldrin struggled into their bulky space suits and prepared to step out on to the moon.

SAFELY BACK TO EARTH

July 24, USS *Hornet*, Pacific Ocean The Columbia splashed down into the Pacific earlier today. President Nixon is here on board the aircraft carrier *Hornet* to welcome the returned astronauts. But no one, not even the President of the United States, is allowed to shake their hands or meet them face to face. The astronauts are wearing special clothing and are living in a sealed container. They will stay there until tests prove that they did not pick up some deadly infection during their visit to the moon.

Edwin 'Buzz' Aldrin walks on the moon. Neil Armstrong is reflected in his helmet.

A VIEW FROM THE MOON

July 21, The moon "The sky is black, you know . . . It's a peculiar thing, but the surface looked very warm and inviting."

Neil Armstrong

"Still don't know exactly what colour to describe this other than greyish-cocoa colour. It appears to be covering most of the lighter part of my boot . . . very fine particles. . ."

Edwin Aldrin

(From *First on the Moon*, Farmer and Hamblin, Michael Joseph 1970)

MOON PROGRAMME QUESTIONED

Dec 31, Washington The second moon-shot last month was another technical triumph. The craft managed to land within 1000 m of an unmanned moon probe sent up in 1967. The astronauts collected 34 kg of rock and set up several experiments. Amazingly clear pictures of the moon were beamed back to TV sets on earth. But the future of the moon programme is uncertain. A fifth of the world's population watched the first moon landing but since then it seems that nobody is interested in space any more. Many scientists doubt that the benefits to science of the moon landings are worth the colossal cost.

NEWS IN BRIEF . . .

CZECHOSLOVAKIA MOURNS A MARTYR

Jan 25, Prague On January 19, Jan Palach, a 21-year-old student, burned himself to death in Prague's Wenceslas Square. His suicide was a protest against the Soviet occupation of his country. When he was buried today, hundreds of thousands of Czechs lined the streets of Prague to pay tribute to his sacrifice.

Jan Palach's grave in Prague

NEW LEADER FOR PALESTINE GUERRILLAS

Feb 3, Cairo The new head of the Palestine Liberation Organization is to be the guerrilla leader, Yasser Arafat. Mr. Arafat is a Palestinian; he was born in Jerusalem in 1929. In 1963 he founded the Al Fatah movement to win back Palestine from the Israelis.

Mr. Yasser Arafat

OIL FOUND UNDER THE NORTH SEA

June 25, London A company drilling for oil in the rocks under the British sector of the North Sea has confirmed that high-quality oil has been found. The strike lies in deep water, way out in one of the worst storm areas of the North Sea.

BRITAIN GOES DECIMAL

Oct 21, London August 1972 is the deadline for Britain's changeover to a decimal coinage. Last year the 10 pence coin came out. Today the seven-sided 50 pence piece appears. Still to come are the ½p, 1p, 2p and 5p coins.

THE MAXI LOOK

Oct 21, Paris The sixties will go down in fashion history as the decade of the mini-skirt. But now the mini is dead. There was not a knee to be seen at the fashion shows here this autumn. The new 'maxi' skirt ends just above the ankle and the audience loved it. It is worn with boots and an ankle-length coat.

PEOPLE OF THE SIXTIES

John Fitzgerald Kennedy 1917 - 63

After winning medals for bravery in World War II, John Kennedy entered politics. In 1960 he was elected President of the United States. Aged 43, he was the youngest person and the first Roman Catholic to hold the office. He won the admiration and gratitude of the free world for his handling of the 1962 Cuban missile crisis and for his stand against the Soviet Union. Kennedy was assassinated in Dallas in 1963.

Martin Luther King 1929 - 68

Dr. King was a leading religious and civil rights campaigner in the United States. A Baptist minister like his father, Dr. King became a leader of America's black people in their struggle to win equal rights with the whites. He was awarded the Kennedy Peace Prize and, in 1964, the Nobel Peace Prize. He was murdered by a white racist in 1968. His memory continues to inspire black people throughout the world.

Lyndon Baines Johnson 1908 - 73

As US Vice-President, Lyndon Johnson became President when John Kennedy was assassinated in 1963. He was re-elected to the Presidency in 1964. Johnson was in power when laws were passed which improved the position of black people in America but was blamed for the US failure to win the war in Vietnam. His unpopularity caused him to give up politics in 1968.

Nikita Sergeyevich Khrushchev 1894 - 1971

Nikita Khrushchev was born near Kursk and joined the Communist Party in 1918. He became prime minister of the Soviet Union shortly after the death of Stalin. His attempt to set up nuclear missiles in Cuba almost led to war with the United States. After the crisis was over he adopted a more friendly approach towards the Western powers. His softer policies won him many powerful enemies in the Soviet Union and they turned him out of office in 1964.

Muhammad Ali, boxer 1942 -

Ali began his career as Cassius Clay, but changed his name to Muhammad Ali when he converted to the Black Muslim faith. In 1964 he beat Sonny Liston to become World Heavyweight Champion. Ali became a hero to sports fans and black people everywhere. He supported the black rights movement and opposed the war in Vietnam. When he refused to fight in the war he was arrested and stripped of his title. He returned to the ring and regained the title in 1974, and again in 1978.

Alexander Dubcek 1921 -

Alexander Dubcek became leader of the Czechoslovakian Government in 1968. When he lifted censorship and began to introduce freedoms of other kinds in Czechoslovakia, Soviet troops invaded the country and put an end to his reforms. Dubcek was disgraced and forced out of politics. He returned to public life and was honoured as a pioneer of Czech freedom when the Communist Government was overthrown in 1989.

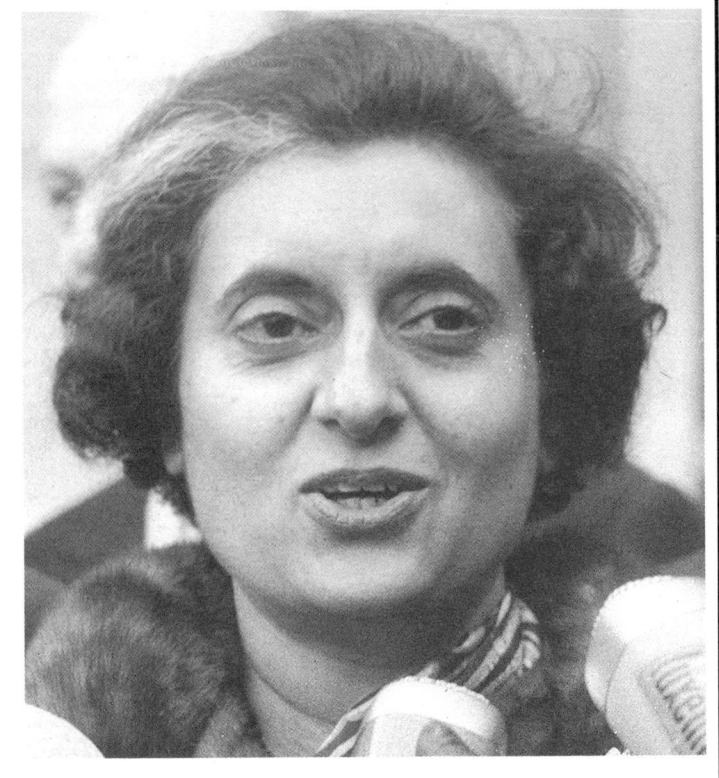

Indira Gandhi 1917 - 84

Indira Gandhi was the daughter of Jawaharlal Nehru, the first Prime Minister of India after independence. She joined her father's Congress Party and worked with him in the struggle to free India from British rule. She was elected to Parliament and in 1959 became President of the Congress Party. In 1964, after her father died, she entered the Cabinet as Minister of Information. Two years later she became India's third Prime Minister and went on to serve as India's Prime Minister four times. In 1984 she was assassinated by her Sikh bodyguard.

Billie Jean King 1943 -

Billie Jean King was born Billie Jean Moffitt in California. At school she was good at all games but took up tennis when she was given a cheap $8 tennis racket. In her long career, Billie Jean won over 50 championships including 20 at Wimbledon. When she became a top-ranking player in the sixties, men players were paid more than twice as much as women. Mrs. King campaigned hard for equal pay for women. Thanks to her efforts, men and women players are now treated equally.

For the first time ever

1960	USA	First vaccinations against measles
		Laser developed
	UK	Artificial ski slope opened
		Portacabin on sale
		Jump jet revealed
	Japan	Fibre-tip pen on sale
		First all-transistor TV
1961	USA	Electric toothbrush on sale
		First golfball electronic typewriter
		First radio broadcast in stereo
	Switzerland	Valium developed
	France	Hatchback car – Renault 4 – on sale
	UK	Zone-toughened car windscreen available
1962	Japan	Micro-television receiver in use
	USA	Telstar communications satellite
		Minicomputer on sale
	UK	Passenger hovercraft in use
1963	UK	Rotary lawnmower (Flymo) on sale
	USA	Navigation satellite launched
1964	USA	Programmers use BASIC computer language
		Eye surgeons use laser
		Fibreglass sailboard on sale
		Music syntheziser in use
	Japan	Home video recorder developed
1965	USA	Global communications satellite launched
		Mass-produced minicomputer on sale
		Word processor available
	France	Radial tyre (Michelin) on sale
	UK	Pilots use automatic aircraft landing system

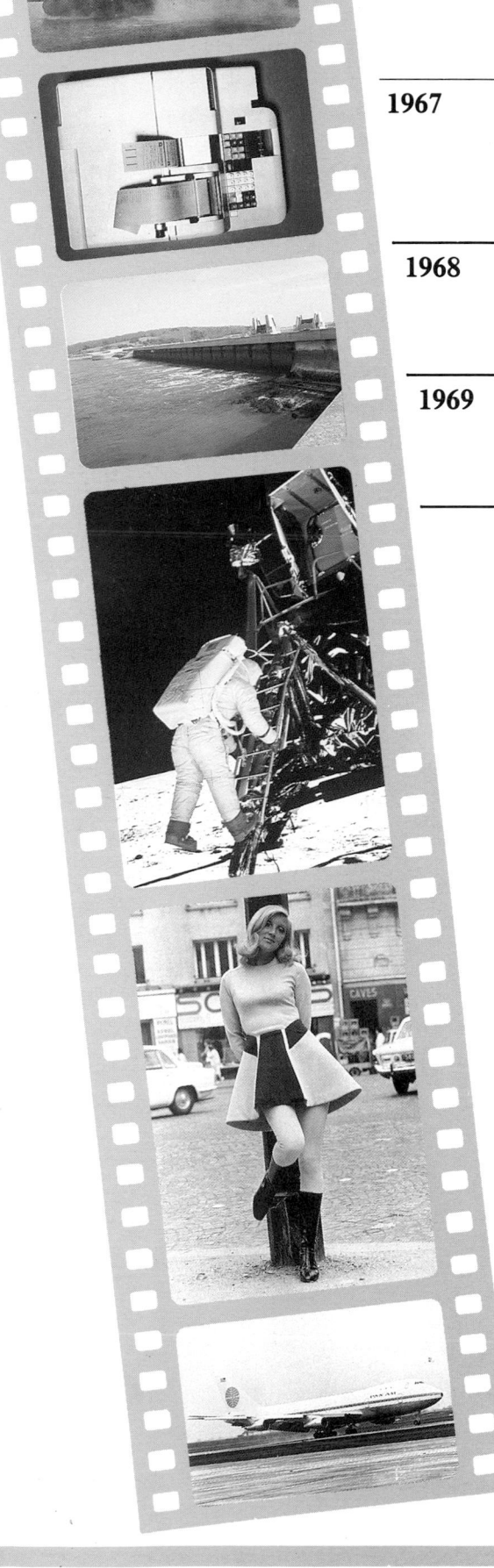

1966	USA	Every child wants a skateboard
	UK	Dolby noise reduction system in use
		Optical fibre telephone cable developed
	Japan	A supertanker is launched
		Integrated circuit radio available
1967	Germany	A car engine has fuel injection
	France	Tidal electric power station in operation
	South Africa	A human heart is transplanted
1968	UK	Astronomers discover pulsars
	USSR	Supersonic airliner flown
	Japan	Trinitron colour television tube used
1969	USA	Jumbo-jet test flight (Boeing 747)
	Switzerland	PASCAL computer language used
	Japan	Video-cassette system on sale

New words and expressions

New words and expressions are constantly being added to the English language. Many of those which appeared for the first time in the sixties arose from rock music, space travel, computers and war.

body count	Op Art
disaster area	reclosable
ego trip	returnable
flower-power/people	rip-off
go-go dancing	shrink-wrap
groupie	soft-landing
hands-on	solar panel
hangup	space shuttle
hardline	space walk
hard rock	spaced out
keypad	underfund
mainframe	update
meltdown	uptight
microchip	urban sprawl
mind-blowing	value-added tax
name of the game	wheeler-dealer
networking	world-class
nuke	

How many of these words and expressions do we still use today? Do you know what they all mean?

Glossary

apartheid: the policy of the South African Nationalist Party, of keeping white people apart from people of other races and giving them many privileges.

black power: in the 1960s the black peoples of America grouped themselves together to fight for equality with the whites. They called their combined strength 'black power'.

call-up: an official order to join the army, navy or airforce.

civil rights: the rights that people have to the same treatment and opportunities, no matter what their race, religion or sex may be.

colony: a territory governed and controlled by people from another country.

commission of enquiry: a group of people appointed by a government to examine a particular problem and make a report on it.

contraception: any method of preventing pregnancy resulting from sexual intercourse; birth control.

fall-out: pieces of radioactive material produced by a nuclear explosion.

federal marshal: an officer appointed by the government to keep law and order.

guerrilla: someone who fights as part of an irregular army, not part of the official forces of the state; (from a Spanish word meaning 'little war').

Indo-China: in south-east Asia the countries of Laos, Cambodia and Vietnam together make up an area called Indo-China.

Palestine: the Arab name for a country at the eastern end of the Mediterranean. The Jews call it Israel.

pass laws: in South Africa the laws which compelled non-white people to carry passes to enable them to travel about in their own country. Pass laws were one of the main features of apartheid.

Queen's Birthday Honours List: In Britain, honours such as knighthoods and medals for services to the country are awarded twice a year. The first occasion is on New Year's Day; the second is on a day in mid-June known as the Queen's Official Birthday.

Rhodesia: Northern and Southern Rhodesia were the former names of two British colonies in southern Africa. On gaining independence, Northern Rhodesia became Zambia. Southern Rhodesia took the name Zimbabwe.

regime: a system or method of government e.g. a fascist regime.

sabotage: deliberate damage done to something such as piece of machinery to stop it working.

sanctions: if one country has broken international law, other countries may combine to stop its trade and prevent other contacts with the outside world. These punishments are called sanctions.

summit: a meeting between the top leaders of nations, rather than just their ministers.

Third World: countries in Africa, Asia and South America which are poor and under-developed.

townships: areas on the outskirts of South African towns where most non-white people have been obliged to live. Sharpeville was a township near Vereeniging south of Johannesburg.

Further reading

The Twentieth Century World: Peter and Mary Speed. Oxford University Press 1982

Portrait of a Decade series; *The 1960s*: Trevor Fisher. Batsford 1988

Living Through History series; *The 1960s*: Elizabeth Campling. Batsford 1988

The 1960s: R. G. Grant. Bison Books 1990

Great Lives of the Twentieth Century: Ed. Alan Bullock. Weidenfeld 1981

Mao: Frederick King Poole. Watts 1982

The Middle East: Charles Messenger. Watts 1987

Vietnam: Ed. John Pimlott. Macdonald 1988

Chronicle of the 20th Century: Ed. Derrik Mercer. Longman 1988